Table Of Contents

The Kariye (Chora) Museum 5

The Architecture 8

Plan of the Kariye (Chora) Museum 12

Virgin Mary's visit to Bethlehem (A-1) 14

Virgin Mary, Joseph and the enrollment for the census for taxation (A-2)........................... 16

Jesus going together with Mary and John to Jerusalem on Easter (A-3) 17

The birth of Christ (B-6) 18

The return of the Virgin Mary and Jesus from Egypt to Nazareth (B-7) 19

Attempts by Satan to deceive Jesus (B-8) 20

Consecration by Jesus (C-10) 23

The prayer of Mary and the Angels (C-11) 24

Water being turned into wine (C-12) 26

Three Magi from the East in audience with King Herod (D-14) 28

Elizabeth and John flee away from a pursuing soldier (D-15) 30

King Herod's order for the massacre of the innocents (F-24) 32

Jesus and his ancestors (Genealogy of Christ) (J-27) 34

The mosaics of the Khalke Jesus and Mary (J-33) 40

Mary and the child Jesus (G-34) 44

Mary and Joseph bidding each other farewell (G-39) 46

Blessing of the Virgin Mary (H-42) 50

Joseph and the stick that indicates Mary as his fiancé (H-43) 52

The birth of the Virgin (H-44) 53

The mosaics of the apostles St. Paul and St. Peter 55

The Virgin taking the skeins of wool, to weave the veil for the temple (I-47) 56

The feeding of the Virgin by an angel (I-J-49) . 58

Presentation of the church by Theodore Metochites to Jesus (I-48) 59

The death of the Virgin (50-a) 62

Plan of the Parecclesion 64

The frescoes of the Parecclesion 66

Fresco of the Anastasis (1) 68

The Last Judgement scene (6) 72

The Virgin and the attendant twelve angels in the dome 74

Published and distributed by:

AKŞİT KÜLTÜR ve TURİZM YAYINCILIK

Cağaloğlu Yokuşu, Cemal Nadir Sok. Nur İşhanı, 2/4 34440 Cağaloğlu / İstanbul - TURKEY Tel: (+90- 212) 511 53 85 - 511 67 82 Fax: 527 68 13 www.aksityayincilik.com

Text by	: İlhan Akşit
Translated by	: Uluer Bilgen
Pictures by	: Tahsin Aydoğmuş,
Composed by	: Nilgün Çifter
Graphics by	: Gülten Aksu
Colour seperation by	: Ram Renk Ayrımı
Printed in Turkey by	: Seçil Ofset, 0212 629 06 15

A general view of the Kariye Museum.

4

The Museum of Chora
Mosaics and Frescoes

Archaeologist
İlhan Akşit

akşit

KÜLTÜR TURİZM SANAT AJANS VE TİC. LTD. STİ.

In the dome, Jesus and his ancestors; below, the Virgin and Jesus.   2

The Kariye (Chora) Museum

The Kariye Museum, in which we regard the mosaics with a deep sense of admiration, is situated in the Edirnekapı quarter of Istanbul. The name of Kariye is derived from the Greek word "Chora", which means land, country, a suburb or suburban area, as well as countryside. The Monastery of Chora was thus named, as it lied outside of the city walls built by the Emperor Constantine. Although the monastery lied within the walls built by the Emperor Theodosius in 413 A.D., its name still remained unchanged and it was referred to as the Chora. During the reign of Emperor Justinian, the monastery was devastated by an earthquake on October 6, 557. The Emperor had then rebuilt the monastery as a basilica. The monastery was again in ruins in the VIII. Century and it was restored again in 843 A.D. After that, the history of the Chora Monastery lies in profound darkness until the 11th Century.

During the Kommenos dynasty, the monastery was again in a heap of ruins. We know that it was restored and rebuilt by Maria Dukaena, the mother-in-law of the Emperor Alexios I. Komnenos (1081-1118), the third son of Alexios Komnenos, who was the grandson of Maria Dukaena, has taken part in the restoration activities, and hence he was depicted just beside the Virgin in the panel of Jesus Christ and the Virgin Mary.

During the 57 years long duration of the occupation of Istanbul by the Latins from 1204 up to 1261,

The Virgin and the child Jesus, in the apse of the nave.

although all the churches in Istanbul were in ruins, this church was not even occupied. The Monastery, which later was in the possession of Orthodox priests, was again in ruins, because of the negligence in maintenance.

At that time, the Byzantine Emperor Mikhail Palaiologos VIII. (1259) had formed a government in Nicea. Upon returning to Istanbul, he has tried with other prominent state authorities, to repair and restore churches that were in ruins.

Theodore Metochites, who was a poet and a man of letters, as well as being an auditor of the treasury during the reign of Andronikos II (1282-1328), was living in the same neighbourhood. Metochites restored the monastery in an excellent manner. Theodore was born in Nicea into a poor family. As he was very intelligent and industrious, he studied political science and literature in Byzantium. He succeeded to provide his children with a very good education. Metochites, being a scholar and a humanitarian, dedicated his intelligence and fortune to the restoration of this monastery and church. Without touching the dome, he had a narthex built in front of the building and added a chapel in the east. He had the entire structure adorned with mosaics and frescoes in 1312. The building structure that survived to our era is from that epoch.

Andronikos III, who succeeded Andronikos II, sent Metochites into exile to Didymoteichos in Western Thrace, for the simple reason of his being loyal to the former emperor. Metochites lived

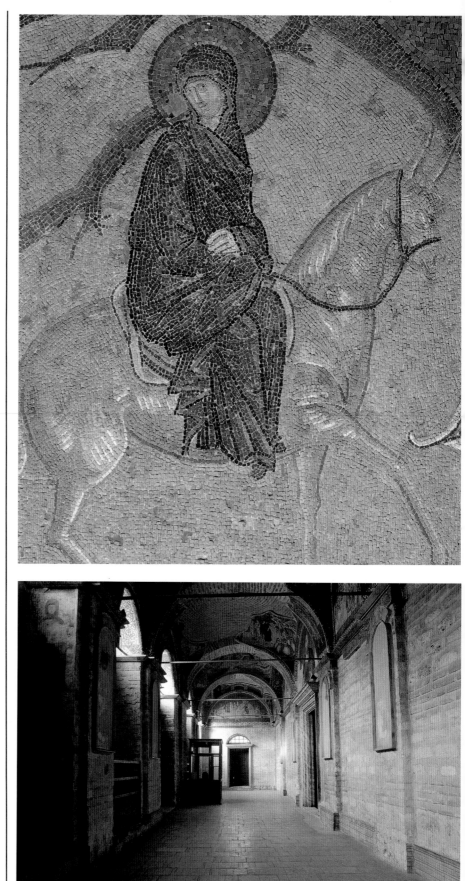

Detail showing the Virgin, from the panel of the voyage to Bethlehem.

View of the first narthex.

6

A rear view of the Kariye Museum.
General view of the second narthex.

there in exile, for a long time until being pardoned, and he returned to Byzantium a sick and poor man. He then took shelter as a priest in the church he had restored, and died there in 1332.

After the conquest of Istanbul by the Turks in 1453, the Chora Monastery was converted into a mosque in 1511 by Atik Ali Paşa, the Grand Vizier of Sultan Bayazıt II. No interference was made to the architecture, except the addition of a minaret, and the name of the Chora monastery became Kariye since then, and it became known as the Kariye Mosque.

After the conversion of the mosque into a museum, it was repaired by the American Byzantine Institute from 1948 to 1958.

The plasters and white-wash covering the mosaics and frescoes were removed and cleaned, and its present day outlook was restored through the fulfillment of the necessary restoration work.

The Architecture

As the building consisted of an apse and a narthex in its initial construction, in later repairs and additions the main structure was kept intact; only an annex was made in the north of the structure, an outer narthex in the west, and a long and slender chapel was added in later years. This chapel is a long and slender building with a dome and is constructed over the cellar. The East end ends with an apse. All the round arches, semi-supports, niches in the outer fronts of the building, as well as the masonry and brick-laying workmanship contribute motion to the outer look of the building and save it from being a massive block.

The present building covers an area of 27.5 meters by 27 meters. The length of the Parecclesion is 29 m. The church has six domes, of which the greatist lies in the center with a diameter of 7.70 m. Two domes are located in the inner narthex, and the other two are situated at the right and left of the apse. The second greatest dome after the central one, is located in the Parecclesion, with a diameter of 4.50 meters. The apse has three windows. The main building is covered with marbles of wonderful colours. The inner narthex is of 4 m. width and of 18 m. length. There is a door from here leading to the Parecclesion. The outer narthex is of 4 m. width and 23.30 m. length. The niches in the outer

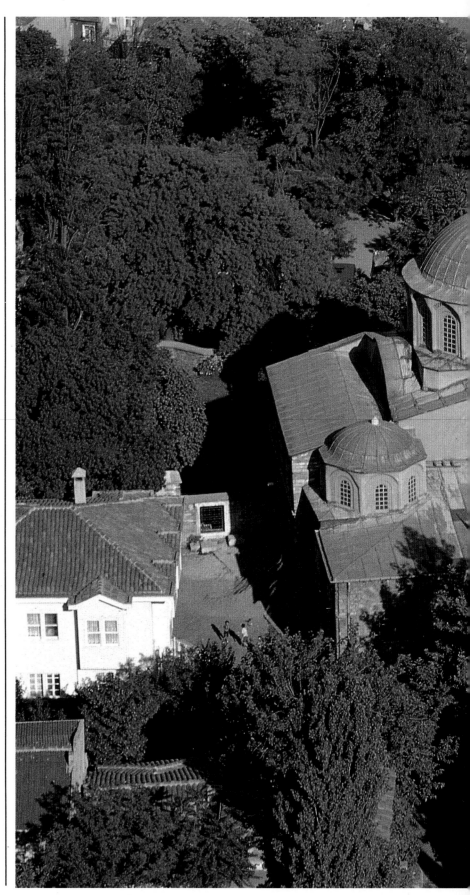

An aerial view of the Kariye Museum.

A view of the main section of the Chora.

Stone panel over the Virgin.

narthex and in the annexed chapel have been used as tombs. The mosaics were made by drawing draft pictures on a fast drying plaster and sticking over them coloured pieces of stones, bricks and glass. As gold was also used in the mosaics during the reign of Emperor Justinian, magnificient pieces of art had been created. In the XIV; Century during the Palaiologos dynasty, the art of mosaic ornamentation has displayed a great development in Istanbul. The Chora Monastery

built in this period is the most important evidence to this.

The themes dealt with in the inner and outer narthexes follow each other periodically just like the serial sequences of a comics book. On the northern wing of the inner narthex eighteen incidents describing the life story of the Virgin are depicted with all its beauty.

On the north of the outer narthex, important events in the lives of the holy family and the birth and baptizing of Christ are dealt with. The miracles of Jesus and his other deeds while diffusing the Words of God are dealt in the southern wings of both narthexes. But, because of the fall of the plasters, many of the important mosaics have not survived our epoch.

The short inscriptions seen on the mosaics are either symbols or writings explanatory to the mosaics. A harmonious blend of colours made in a natural way, creates a sense of admiration in those, who have the chance of looking at them.

We shall not follow the chronological order, but simply starting from the left of the enterance door, we shall see the wonderful mosaics in the outer narthex first, by following the numbers in our plan. Then, we shall conclude the tour of the museum, by visiting the inner narthex and the main section, and later on by visiting the annexed chapel.

A side view of the Kariye Museum.

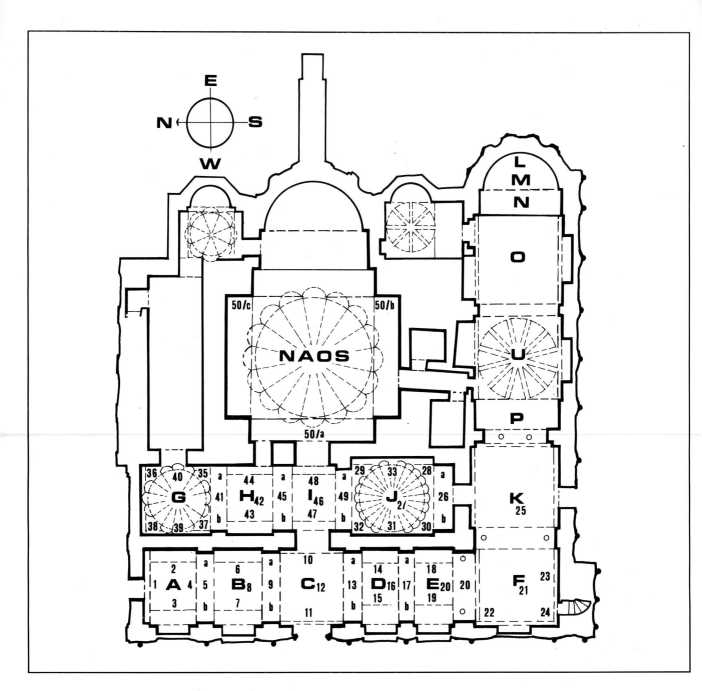

Plan of the Kariye (Chora) Museum

A 1- The voyage of the Virgin to Bethlehem and the dream of Joseph.
2- The census held for the enrollment for taxation and registration of Mary and Joseph in the presence of Cyrenius, the Governor of Syria.
3- Jesus going together with Mary and Joseph to Jerusalem, on Easter.
4- Remains of mosaics-Jesus among the doctors in the temple.
A.B 5- a) St Trachos b) St Andronikus
6- The birth of Jesus.

7- The return of the Virgin Mary with Jesus.
8- The attempts of Satan to deceive Jesus.
B.C 9- a) St Georgios b) St Demetrius.
C 10- Jesus and the inscription; "the dwelling-place of the living"
11- The prayer of the Virgin and the attendent angels.
12- The wedding at Cana and the miracles.
C.D 13- a) and b) Depiction of the saints.
D 14- The Magi on their way to Jerusalem riding on horseback and the three Magi in audience with King Herod.

15- Elizabeth and John the Baptist running away from a pursuing soldier.
16- Remains of mosaics.
D.E 17- a) and b) Depiction of the saints.
E 18- The scene of King Herod's investigation and a guard standing.
19- The mourning mothers.
E.F 20- No mosaics are left.
21- A decorative medallion.
22- The meeting of Jesus with the Samaritan woman at the well.
23- The healing by Jesus, of a paralyzed person

12

24- King Herod giving the order for the massacre of the innocents and the execution thereof.

K 25- Remains of mosaics.

K.J 26- a) The healing by Jesus of a young man with an injured arm.
b) The healing by Jesus Christ, of the leprous man.

J 27- Twenty-four of the early ancestors of Jesus Christ (Genealogy of Christ).

28- The healing by Christ, of a woman asking for a restoration of her health.

29- The healing by Jesus Christ, of the mother-in-law of St. Peter.

30- The healing by Jesus Christ of a deaf person.

31- Dispersion of good health by Jesus Christ to the people.

32- The healing by Jesus Christ, of two blind men.

33- The Khalke Jesus and the praying Virgin.

G 34- The Virgin and the child Jesus.

35- Joachim in the mountains praying for having a child.

36- No mosaics are left.

37- The breaking of the good news of the birth of Jesus to Mary-The Anunciation

38- The chief priest Zacchariah judging the Virgin.

39- Mary and Joseph bidding each other farewell.

40- The breaking of the good news of the birth of Mary to Anne-The Anunciation.

G.H 41- a) The meeting of Anne and Joachim.
b) Joseph bringing the Virgin into his house

H 42- Mary in the arms of Anne and Joachim, and the blessing by the priests.

43- Giving of the stick with young shoots, indicating Joseph as Mary's fiancé.

44- The birth of the Virgin Mary.

H.I 45- a) The first seven steps of the Virgin, and below, St. Peter.
b) The prayer of the chief priest Zacchariah in front of the twelve sticks.

I 46- The presentation of Mary (aged three) to the temple by her parents.

47- The Virgin taking the skeins of wool to weave the veil for the temple.

48- Theodore Metochites presenting a small model of the church to Jesus Christ.

I.J 49- a) The feeding of the Virgin by an angel, and below, St. Peter.
b) Remains of mosaics - Directives given to the Virgin at the temple.

N 50- a) The death of the Virgin.
b) Mary and the child Jesus.
c) Jesus in a standing posture, holds the Bible in his hand.

St George (B.C 9).

Virgin Mary's visit to Bethlehem (A-1)

Let us start our tour by studying the mosaics on the wall at the furthest left of the outer narthex, that is to say, from the left section of the Kariye Museum. In the section denoted as A in our plan, the mosaics number 1 takes as its subject-matter the Virgin's visit to Bethlehem and Joseph's dream. In this panel of mosaics, three scenes are depicted. On the panel, the person seen sleeping under a small tree is Joseph, Mary's husband. Near him, an angel is breaking him the good news of the approaching birth of Jesus. A little further away from this scene, two women are seen talking to each other: One being Mary, and the other Elizabeth, the wife of Zacchariah. With Joseph walking towards the right, Mary is depicted on horseback, on their journey towards Bethlehem. In the Bible, the birth of Jesus is narrated as follows: Mary and Joseph are engaged, but before they get married, Mary is pregnant. Joseph is very much upset, as he does not know this divine secret. So, begins to consider the breaking up the engagement. While tormenting himself by thinking this unfortunate affair over, he falls asleep and sees an angel in his dream. The angel advises Joseph not to leave his future bride, and that the child is conceived from God Almighty, and soon a boy is to be born, and that he should name this child Jesus. The scene seen at the left of the mosaics depicts this event. When Joseph wakes up, he accept the facts made known to him by the angel, and decides to name the child to be born, Jesus. They continue their journey towards Bethlehem and Jesus is born there.

The voyage of the Virgin to Bethlehem, and a detail from the panel.

Governor Cyrenius, from the panel depicting the census held for the Enrollment for Taxation.

Virgin Mary, Joseph and the enrollment for the census for taxation (A-2)

In this panel of mosaics, located in the north of Section A, the census carried out for the enrollment for taxation is dealt with. The Roman Emperor Augustus has decreed a census all through the Imperial lands. Joseph, who is a descendent of the house of David, takes his fiancé Mary from Nazereth and goes to Bethlehem in the Judea province, for this enrollment. Syria's governor Cyrenius is

The panel of the enrollment for taxation and a detail therefrom.

seated on a chair, with a white headgear on his head, and he is clad in a himation buckled at the shoulder. Behind him stand an armoured guard. At the middle is the official who is in charge of the registration, and another man standing beside him and holding a sword in his hand. The Virgin standing in front of a house with trees and is being enrolled. Joseph seen with a halo over his head, behind him stand his four sons. The inscription of three lines seen at the middle of the panel is an explanation of subjects dealt in the mosaics.

Jesus going together with Mary and John to Jerusalem on Easter (A-3)

Panel of mosaics No. 3, located inside the outer wall at the southern part of section A, takes up as its subject-matter Jesus going together with Mary and John the Baptist to Jerusalem on Easter. On this panel, certain saints like Anempodistus, Epideforous, Alphonius and Pegasius are depicted in medallions. This panel is rather weak in comparison to others. For example, the grace, well-balance

Jesus visiting Jerusalem on Easter and a detail.

and richness observed in the former panel are absent in this one. As the mosaics in the Chora were made by a variety of artists, some are exquisite, while some others, like this one, are rather poor. In this panel, on the right, buildings with large doors and windows are seen. Jesus, Mary and John are here depicted entering Jerusalem. On the left, the entire mosaics in the dome are destroyed. In the section denoted as No. 4 in our plan, Jesus is seen among the doctors in the temple.

The birth of Christ (B-6)

At the place denoted as B-6 in section B, mosaics that depict the birth of Jesus are found. This panel deals with events related to the birth of Jesus.

At the far left, a woman is seen pouring water to a wide basin with high supporting feet. Facing her, another woman is seen seated on a chair, holding the newly-born Jesus in her arms, and wishing to bathe him. In the background, Mary is seen awake and resting after the child-birth. Angels are seen behind Mary.

The birth of Jesus Christ.

St. Tarachos.

Above Mary, a strong and radiant column of light is casted from the sky over Jesus, wrapped in swaddling-clothes. On the right, three shepherds are seen; two seated, and one standing. The angel descending from the sky, is depicted as if saying something to these shepherds.

At the bottom corner Joseph is seen in a sitting position, watching over the bathing of Jesus.

The return of the Virgin Mary and Jesus from Egypt to Nazareth (B-7)

In this section located in the inner surface of the outside wall of the church, the return of the holy family from Egypt is taken up as subject-matter. An angel comes up to Joseph one day during his sleep, and tells him to go to Egypt, taking with him Mary and Jesus, and stay there until the time of return is made known to him. This must be done, because soon King Herod will start a search for the innocent Jesus to

The return of Joseph and Mary to Nazareth from Egypt.

have him killed. Upon this warning Joseph flees to Egypt, taking with him Mary and Jesus. On this panel, the town of Nazareth is seen on the right. On the left, Joseph is seen asleep on a mattress. An angel comes up to the sleeping Joseph and tells him that since King Herod is dead, they may go back to Nazareth. (Matthew 2: 12-22). In the middle a horse is seen ready, together with Mary and Joseph holding Jesus on his shoulders. On the vault (flying buttress), the icons of such saints as Philemon, Calinikus, Tirsus and Apolinus are presented.

Attempts By Satan to deceive Jesus (B-8)

On the ceiling of section B in our museum plan, several attempts by Satan to deceive Jesus are depicted as subject-matter. Around the medallion in the middle, the subjects are developed.

On one of the corners of the dome, the baptizing of Jesus by John the Baptist on the shores of the River Jordan can be seen. The events following are set in various other parts of the dome.
After the baptizing of Jesus, the Holy Spirit wishes to test Jesus, and birngs him to the desert.
Jesus fasts in the desert forty days and nights, and finally feels hungary.

At this point Satan approaches Jesus and says to him: "As you are the son of God, make some bread.", and whereupon Jesus replies: "Man lives not only on bread, but in every word that God utters."
Upon this, Satan takes Jesus to Jerusalem and places him upon the tower of the temple, and says to him: "As you are the son of God, throw yourself to the ground. Since God ordered his angels to carry you on their hands, your feet then should not touch the stones." Upon these words Jesus replies by saying, "It is written that you should not try your God."

Satan takes Jesus this time to the summit of a high mountain.

The panel depicting the attempts of Satan to deceive Jesus, and a detail therefrom.

The panel depicting the attempts of Satan to deceive Jesus, and a detail.

There, Satan shows him all the countries in the world and their beauties, and tells Jesus that if he kneels down and worships him, he will give Jesus all these countries and their beauties. Jesus says to Satan, "Go away Satan, It is written that you will worship only your own God and be only His creatures." Upon these words, Satan leaves Jesus and goes away. Angels come and serve Jesus. (Matthew 4: 1-11, Mark 1: 12-13, Luke: 1: 1-13).

Consecration By Jesus (C-10)

On the door leading to the inner narthex, just opposite the entrance to the museum, we find a magnificent portrait of Jesus Christ. Upon entering the museum, we are confronted with this splendid mosaic depiction of Jesus. We see Jesus here with a halo over his head, holding the Holy Bible in his left hand and making a sign of blessing with his fingers of his right hand. In this mosaic portrayal, Jesus is depicted having his hair elaborately divided into two sides from the

Jesus over the door leading to the second narthex.

middle of his head, with a spiritual look on his face. To the right of Christ's head and slightly upwards, there is an abbreviation meaning Jesus. And on the inner and left side, stands the abbreviation XC, which is one of the names of Christ. Beneath these, on the right-hand side we read the inscription Hora (Chora) and "Jesus Christ, the dwelling-place of the living" on the left side. Philosophically, this characteristic of Jesus, which is also indicated in the Bible, is thus coupled with the name of the church.

The prayer of Mary and the Angels (C-11)

Upon the entrance door to the Kariye Museum stand portraits of Mary praying and the two angels. Here, at Mary's bosom, a portrait of Jesus with a halo over his head, is seen in a medallion. Mary, in a calm and dignified manner, stands with arms stretched upwards and holding her hands in prayer.

Two angels, each with a halo over its head, stand on both sides of the Virgin; one at the right and one at the left. Against the standing still figure of the Virgin,

Mary over the entrance door to the museum, and a detail therefrom.

the artist has revived the panel by rendering motion to the angels. Most likely this artist was one of the best among the artists, who made the mosaics in the church.

In the inscription on the panel, one reads the words "Mother of God, the dwelling-place of the Never Contained". Between sections C and D, deteriorated saint portraits are found on the arch No. 13.

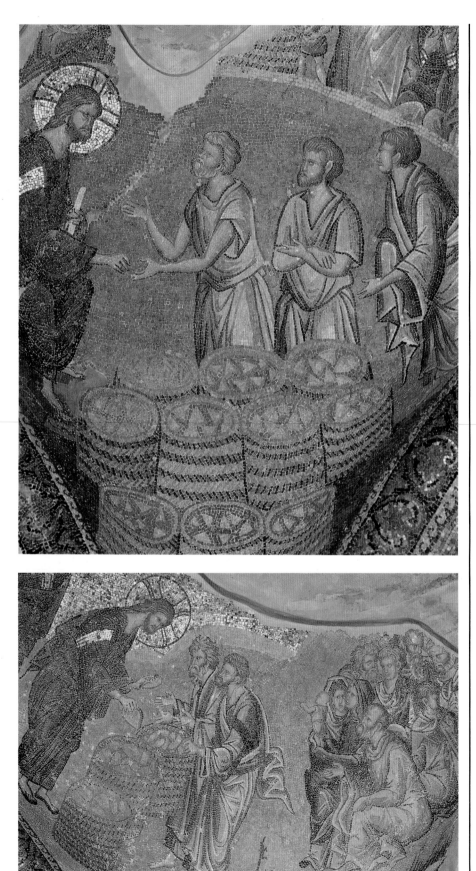

Water being turned into wine (C-12)

On the ceiling located between the door at the entrance to the museum and the door leading to the inner narthex, the miracle of water being turned into wine is depicted.

In the town of Cana in Galilea a wedding party is taking place. Among those invited are Jesus Christ, his apostles and his mother Mary. During the festivities the stocks of wine in the house are depleted. After his mother telling him that "there is no more wine left", Christ orders the servants to fill the six big jars standing there with water. After the jars being filled, Jesus asks them to take a goblet and fill it from one of the jars, and take it to the governor of the wedding. The governor, after taking a sip tells them that there is no water but wine in the goblet, and all those present are astounded, and they restore their faith in Jesus. On the panel of mosaics, this miracle of Jesus is depicted. In front of the jars, the servants are seen carrying water, one empties the pitcher he holds into the jar, and the other servant approaches with a pitcher on his shoulder. At the left side of the panel, we see a group of apostles watching this miracle of Christ with amazment and in awe. Again at this partition, another miracle by Jesus, the sacrifice of a bull is seen. On the south side, such miracles of Jesus like the multiplication of loaves of bread are illustrated. (John 2: 1-10)

Of the miracles performed by Jesus: Multiplication of fish and loaves of bread.

The miracle of water turning into wine

26

Three Magi from the East in audience with King Herod (D-14)

In the mosaics on the inner narthex wall at the immediate right of the museum entrance door, three Magi are depicted in audience with King Herod. Telling him that they have discovered the coming birth of Christ from the stars. King Herod is depicted seated on a throne in front of the door, addressing the Magi. There, a guard is seen behind the King. The artist creating the mosaic picture has depicted the Magi in the front with a white beard, the

The Magi from the East, in audience with King Herod.

One of the saint portraits in the Kariye Museum.

one behind him with a black beard and the third one as a young man. And the shining star in question is seen clearly on the sky. The Magi, who informed King Herod of the natal place, have received an answer such as this: "Go and find me that child. I shall prostrate in reverance to him." But the King shall never keep his promise. Beehind the three Magi, a composition of other Magi are seen riding on horseback, headed for Jerusalem.

King Herod's investigation and a standing guard.

Elizabeth and John flee away from a pursuing soldier (D-15)

On the right of the entrance door and on the inner surface of the outer wall of the church, Elizabeth and John are depicted as they run away from a soldier chasing them with a sword in his hand. Elizabeth is a relative of the Virgin and she is the wife of Zacchariah, and the mother of John the Baptist. On the arch No. 17 between sections D and E on the side, there are portraits of the saints. But since the mosaics have

The flight of Elizabeth and John the Baptist from a pursuing soldier.

Details from the massacre of the children

fallen, it is not possible to identify them. Panel No. 18 on the inner narthex wall in section E is also highly deteriorated. A guard is seen interrogating a woman. As it was made known to King Herod that a new born child would overturn his throne, therefore, he issued an order for the killing of all the new born babies. Opposite these, the mourning mothers are depicted. In the middle, on the side arch, there are no mosaics left. Here, only in the point designated as E-18, King Herod is shown while sitting on his throne, with a guard standing behind him.

A detail from the flight of Elizabeth and John. (above)

King Herod's order for the massacre of the innocents (F-24)

On the eastern wall of the outer narthex of the museum, King Herod is depicted while giving orders for the massacre of the innocents. Some Magi inform the King that a child is born in Bethlehem and that this child will lead the Israel nation. These Magi are sent to Bethlehem in search of this child. After the Magi have seen the infant and Mary there, they are notified in their dreams

Healing of a paralyzed person by Christ.

Execution of the order given by King Herod.

that night not to return to King Herod. The obeying Magi go back to their own countries. An angel that Joseph has seen in his dream warns him that King Herod will have the child killed and advise him that they therefore must flee to Egypt. Joseph, flees to Egypt taking with him Mary and the infant Jesus. The king, not being able to find the infant and understanding that he was betrayed by the Magi, gives orders that all chidren below two years of age in Bethlehem and its vicinity be killed. (Matthew 2: 16)

The mosaics in question deal with this subject. The king is seated on a high throne, and is giving orders to the soldiers facing him.

King Herod giving orders for the massacre of the innocents.

The healing of a young man with an injured arm, by Jesus Christ.

On the other side of the mosaics, the execution of this order and the distress of the mothers are shown. Opposite the location of these mosaics, a Samaritan woman is depicted beside a well. Jesus, while passing through Samaria comes across this woman at the well. (F-23) In this section, there is a decorative medallion at the middle of the dome. In section K. no mosaics are in existence. On the arch situated between sections J and K, the healing by Christ of a sick youth and again healing of the leper, are depicted. (Matthew 2: 16)

Jesus and his ancestors (Genalogy of Christ) (J-27)

Within the dome in this section, Jesus is in the middle, surrounded by his ancestors. Jesus in the middle holds in his left hand the Holy Bible and raising his right hand to the level of his chest, makes a sign of blessing with his fingers. In separate sections placed around a wide circle and continuing up to the level of the windows in the dome drums are seen twenty-four of the early ancestors of Jesus from Adam to Jacob in the upper zone, and underneath these, the pictures of the fifteen of Jacob's children are to be found in the lower zone. These are very adroitly placed in independent niches. Starting with Adam, the names of the twenty-four ancestors of Christ are as follows: Adam, Jacob, Adam, Seth, Noah,Cainan, Maleleel, Jared, Lamech, Sem, Japheth, Arphaxand, Saruch, Nachor, Thara, Abraham, Isaac, Jacob, Phalec, Ragau, Enoch, Enos and Abel. These names are written over the heads of the figures.

At the corners of the dome, where the ancestors of Jesus are located, the mosaics of the Khalke Jesus and Mary are to be found, and between this and the arch designated as J-28 on the plan, we see a woman bleeding for years and healed immeadiately after touching the garments of Jesus. On the other corner, we see the healing by Jesus, of the mother-in-law of the Apostle Peter. (J-29). Opposite this, we see the healing of two blind men by Jesus, and in the other, the healing of the deaf. In the wide

In the dome, Jesus Christ and his ancestors.

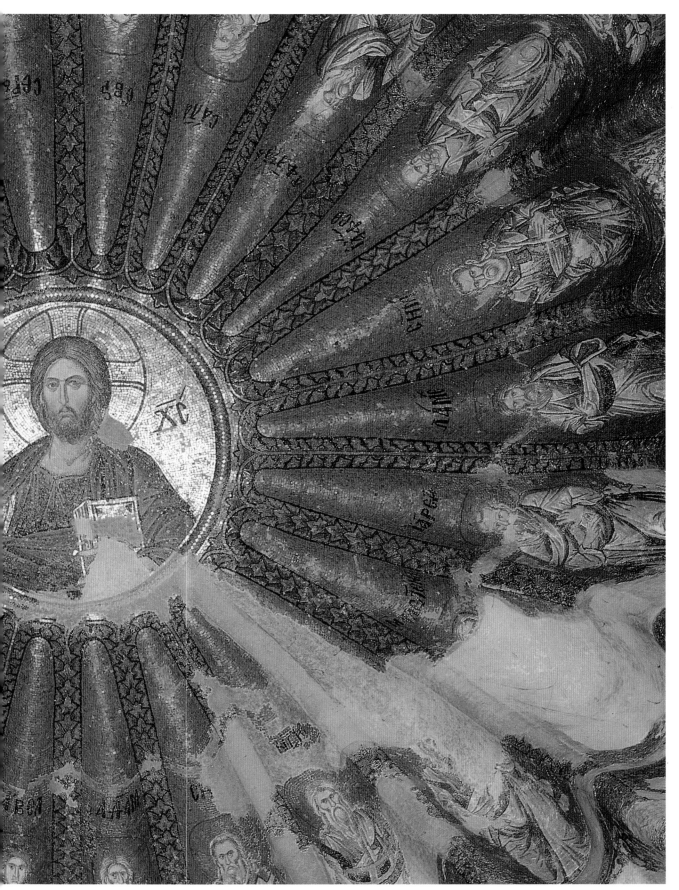

A general view of the dome depicting the genalogy of Christ.

Jesus healing a sick woman asking for a restoration to her former good health.

panel underneath the healing of the sick people with various diseases are seen. The events take place in a village. Men and women, all the sick population of the village have come to Jesus, to seek the restoration to their health. In the panel of mosaics Jesus stands up, clad in a dark garment, leaning forward and stretching a hand in a gesture of healing towards the sick in the foreground, while his apostles are standing behind him. In the background, other sick people awaiting their turn, and a woman clad in a dark robe, bringing her sick child, are seen.

Jesus Christ within the medallion in the dome.

Christ healing various sick people,
and a detail.

Healing of the two blind men.

ΟΧ ΕΙΩΜΕΝΟΣ ΤΙΝ ΠΕΝΘΕΡΑΝ ΠΕΤΡΟ

ΙC ΧC

Healing of the mother-in-law of the apostle Peter.
Healing of the deaf. (below)
The procession of the Virgins. (on the right)

The mosaics of the Khalke Jesus and Mary (J-33)

At the site where Jesus and his ancestors are seen at the dome, there stand mosaics of Jesus and Mary on a large panel on the wall.

Despite the fact that some of the mosaics at the bottom have fallen away, a splendid mosaics of Jesus is confronted here. Under Mary, who is engaged in prayer, Prince Isaac Komnenos is seen kneeling down.

On the right of Jesus, we see Melane, a nun and the daughter of Mikhael Palaiologos VIII. This princess had wed Alaba Khan, a Mongol prince, and after the decease of her husband, she returned to Istanbul and became a nun.

Beside her, there is an inscription "Melane, Lady of the Mongols". These two names must have contributed to the restoration of the church in the 12th Century.

The reason for denoting Jesus as Khalke Jesus, is that this panel was inspired by the icon of a large size found at the entrance to the Khalke Palace in Byzantium.

The panel depicting the Khalke Jesus and the Virgin.

IC XC

The portraits of Jesus of Khalke, Mary and Isaac Komnenos.

The Virgin in the dome and figures representing her ancestors.

Joachim in the mountains praying to have a child, and a detail therefrom.

Mary and the child Jesus (G-34)

There are two domes in the inner narthex of the Kariye Museum. Of these two, on the right dome Jesus and his ancestors are seen and on the left dome, which is smaller, with a diameter of 3.40 meters, Mary and her ancestors are presented. In the middle of the dome Mary is seen holding the child Jesus. Around this medallion we find the ancestors of Mary in 16 sections. These consist of the figures of David and 15 kings. They are David, Solomon, Roboam, Abia, Asa, Josaphat, Joram, Ozias, Joatham, Acnaz, Ezekias, Manasses, Amon, Josias, Jechonias, Salathiel and all of them are in the upper zone. In the lower zone, we see figures of another generation and namely Hananiah, Azariah, Michael, Daniel, Johua, Moses, Aaron, Hur, Samuel, Job and Melchizedek. The letters MP and OV that are located on both sides of the head of Mary, placed in the medallion, are abbreviations used in denoting the title of "Mother of God." Under this dome, denoted as G-35 in our plan, we see Joachim among the bushes in the mountain, praying to have a child. Joachim is Mary's father, and is in distress, because he has no children. Joachim is seen seated on grass in a mountainside, and with a worried look on his face, he is complaining of his bad lot, to the approaching children, carrying sacks on their backs. On the opposite corner (No. 37), the Archangel Gabriel is coming towards Mary at the well, and giving her the good news of the coming birth of Jesus, is depicted. Mary is seen looking with fearful eyes up in the air. Next to this scene, we see Mary and Joseph bidding each other farewell.

The Virgin and her ancestors.

Mary and Joseph bidding each other farewell (G-39)

Joseph is seen with a child near him and bidding farewell to Mary. On the panel, we see big buildings in the background and Joseph in the middle, with a halo over his head. Joseph is raising his right hand in a gesture of greeting Mary, and is walking away. Mary stands in a manner showing her sadness, twisting her head and crossing her arms. Someone carrying a basket watches over this scene. At the corner designated as No. 38, next to this farewell scene, Zacchariah is seen. The complementary part in which

Mary and Joseph bidding each other farewell, and a detail therefrom.

Mary was depicted and the mosaics opposite are destroyed. On the adjacent panel of mosaics No. 40, the breaking of the good news to Anne, Mary's mother, of the coming birth of Mary is taken up as its subject-matter. While Gabriel announces the coming birth of Jesus to Anne, a servant is seen listening to them. On the arch (41-a) between section C and the adjacent section H, such scenes as the meeting of St. Anne with Joachim, and Virgin Mary being led by Joseph to his house, are depicted. In the latter scene, Mary, Joseph and one of Joseph's children are seen.

Breaking the good news to St. Anne, of the coming birth of Mary.

The meeting of St. Anne and Joachim. (below)

The breaking of the good news to the Virgin, of the coming birth of Jesus Christ. (on the right)

Joseph taking the Virgin Mary to his house   48

49   *The presentation of the Virgin Mary to the temple.*

Blessing of the Virgin Mary (H-42)

At the ceiling of the second section at the left of the second narthex, various scenes are being depicted. At one side of the medallion, on the ceiling, child Mary is seen between her parents. Anne and Joachim are seated facing each other, and are caressing Mary. A young girl stretching out of a window, wishes to lean down and reach Mary, in order to take her. A young woman is watching all of this. In the other section, Joachim brings Mary to the clerical leaders for their blessings.

ΗΠΡΟCΤΟΝΙΟCΠΙΤΗΓΑΛΟCΙC

Anne and Joachim caressing the little child Mary.

Bringing of Mary to the temple.

The giving of the verdant stick with young shoots, indicating Joseph as Mary's fiancé.

The peacock figure from the panel depicting Mary's presentation to the temple

Joachim comes up to the spiritual leaders, wearing a tunic with light colours. Three men of the clergy sit around a table awaiting him. The mosaics here which are sound and multi-coloured, are the most dazzling mosaics in the Chora. On the arch located at the flank, the first seven steps of the Virgin Mary, and the chief priest Zacchariah's prayer in front of the twelve sticks are depicted.

Joseph and the stick that indicates Mary as his fiancé (H-43)

On the southern wall in the second section of the inner narthex of the Chora, stand the mosaics that depict the stick that grows green, indicating Mary as Joseph's fiancé. Here, in front of a dais with a four-columned dome on top stands Zacchariah, holding in his right hand a sceptre with young shoots and buds. Mary shall be engaged to the one, whose stick becomes verdant. The stick that Zacchariah holds in his hand belongs to Joseph. As his stick became verdant, he is chosen as Mary's fiancé. Beside Zacchariah stands Mary with a halo over her head. Against them, stands Joseph, and ten aged members of the church are behind him. Zacchariah will hand over Mary to Joseph as his fiancé. As it is widely known, Mary's father Joachim had promised that if he had a child he would bring and leave that child to the temple. He kept his promise and brought his daughter to the temple. Mary, after serving God in the temple for ten years and reaching approximately the age of 14-15, the priests in the temple announced that the time for her marriage had come. The candidates for the future bridegroom shall spend the night at the temple, and the one whose stick becomes verdant and with young shoots, shall be chosen as Mary's fiancé. The candidates assembled in the temple. Finally, the stick of Joseph, who is a carpenter from Nazareth, becomes green with shoots, and he is chosen as Mary's fiancé. This theme is dealt with in the panel of mosaics.

The giving of the verdant stick with young shoots indicating Joseph as Mary's fiancé.

The birth of the Virgin (H-44)

On the wall in the second section at the left in the inner narthex, the theme is Mary's birth. Two young women are seen in front of the door, one of them sitting and holding a new-born baby in her lap. They are trying to bathe the newly born Mary. Joachim is seen watching this scene in amazement, stretching his head and holding a door with his right hand. In the background, we see three women engaged in other everyday chores. Another woman is helping Anne, who lies in bed. Joachim and Anne are Mary's parents. This man and wife, both of whom are descendents of David, were childless. Joachim goes to the temple on a holy day, to make some votive offerings and sacrifices. But the priest sends Joachim away, since he has no children. Joachim then goes up to the mountains and retires with the shepherds of his flocks, and prays there for forty days and nights.

On the last day of the religious festivities, Gabriel pays a visit to Anne, bringing her good tidings; she is soon to have a child. He also tells her that the aged married couple shall one day meet at the Golden Gate in Jerusalem.

Joachim, who is not aware of the good news brought to Anne, offers a sacrifice to God, on the mountain where he retired. The Arcangel Gabriel had announced that one day the old married couple would meet at the Golden

The first seven steps of the Virgin Mary. St. Peter. (below)

Η ΓΕΝΝΗСΙС ΤΗС Α.Κ.

The birth of the Virgin Mary, and a detail therefrom.

Gate in Jerusalem. The old couple meet one day at the Golden Gate. What the Archangel Gabriel has said is materialized. Anne gives birth to a baby girl, whom they call Mary. These are the events that preceded the birth scene depicted in the panel of mosaics. On the adjacent arch, at the point designated as No. 45 in our plan, the panel of mosaics depicting the first seven steps of the Virgin is located. Facing this panel, we see the chief priest Zacchariah praying in front of the twelve sticks.

The mosaics of the apostles St. Paul and St. Peter

On each side of the door leading from the inner narthex to the cella (NAOS), we find the mosaics pertaining to St. Peter and St. Paul. To the right of the door, we see St. Paul in an arched frame. He has a halo over his head and he makes a sign of blessing by raising his right hand to the level of his chest. On the mosaics the inscriptions inform us that St. Paul is represented here. We see him in a natural way, wearing a blue tunic. The mosaics at the bottom have unfortunately fallen. The mosaics panel of St. Paul shows the apostle completely, holding the Holy Bible in his left hand. His facial expression is very successful.

St. Paul was from Tarsus and he belonged to the Jewish race. Later on he became one of the closest disciples of Christ. During the reign of the Roman Emperor Nero (54-68 A.D.), he travelled as far as Rome and upon speaking there about Jesus Christ, he was executed by decapitation. And thus he acquired saintship. On the left side of the door, we find St. Peter. Peter was a man making a living by being a fisherman. One day when he was repairing his fishing nets on the lake shore, he expressed his religious views to Jesus, who came near him by chance. Peter was very much impressed by Jesus, so he became Christ's most faithful disciple since that day. St. Peter is depicted in the panel of mosaics, holding a scroll in his right hand, while in his raised left hand hang two keys; "the keys to the kingdom of heaven".

St. Paul

The Virgin taking the skeins of wool, to weave the veil for the temple (I-47)

Above the door leading from the outer narthex to the inner narthex, we see the representation of the scene of the Virgin taking the skeins of wool to weave the veil for the temple.

At the left of the temple, we see three priests seated on a divan. The priest sitting at the primary position holds in his hand a skein of purple wool. He is giving the wool to the Virgin, who is standing at the middle of the

The Virgin Mary taking the skeins of purple wool to weave the veil for the temple, and a detail therefrom.

The presentation of the Virgin to the temple.

scene, with a halo over her head, clad in a long dress in blue. Behind Mary, stand six virgins attired in colourful costumes, watching over this scene.

The naturalness of the people on the panel, as regards to their standing and behaviour, as well as the beauty and fineness of the composition itself, point out the adroitness and success of the artist, who made the mosaic panel.

The feeding of the Virgin by an angel (I-J 49)

On the arch located at the right of the place leading to the nave, we find the scene depicting the feeding of the Virgin. Mary is seated on a throne at the holy place with four poles. Only the highest priest could enter here once a year. Mary is looking at the angel coming down from the sky and holding a piece of bread in its hand. Mary stretches a hand to receive the piece of bread. Mary's parents had promised that they would give the child to the temple, if they had a child. It is for this reason that Mary was left

Theodore Metochites presenting Jesus a small model of the church.

The feeding of Mary by an angel.

in the custody of the temple. She stayed in the temple for 12 years, until reaching the tender age of 15. Here she was nourished only by the bread brought by the angels. She was engaged to Joseph, whose stick became verdant and with young shoots in a trial contest. Above we see a procession of young virgins at the foot of the dome. These joyful young maidens holding torches in their hands, and whose attires and behaviours display differences, are portrayed in a state of motion.

Presentation of the church by Theodore Metochites to Jesus (I-48)

Above the door leading to the main unit, we see Theodore Metochites presenting Jesus a small model of the church. Jesus Christ is depicted here wearing a loose tunic and seated on a throne.

He is holding with his left hand the Holy Bible lying on his knee-cap, with a sign of the cross on its front cover; and he is making a sign of blessing with his fingers of his right hand raised to the level of his chest. He is seen with a halo over his head, sitting erect, with a sweet look on his face. Facing Christ and kneeling down on the left, holding a small model of the church is Theodore Metochites. He is attired in a moiré robe with full sleeves and long skirts, and ornamented with various designs. He has a long beard and wears a light coloured knitted turban on his head. Although a small model of the church is being presented to Jesus Christ, the artist has not been able to guide Christ's look in the right direction. Perhaps the artist did this on purpose, because of the deep reverance he felt for Jesus. A slight turn of the head would perhaps serve the purpose of this otherwise perfectly depicted scene. As it was pointed out in the former pages, Metochites had the church repaired from the year 1315 up to 1321, and had it embellished with invaluable mosaics and frescoes. Metochites was one of the elites of his epoch, a poet and an astronomer. He was at the same time the Auditor of the Imperial Treasury during the reign of Andronikos II. This quality is made known in the inscriptions found near his head in the illustrations. Above this panel, the scene indicating the presentation of the Virgin in the temple, is located.

Theodore Metochites.

The death of the Virgin (50-a)

In the nave of the church, above the entrance door, we see the death scene of the Virgin. In this scene, Mary is seen lying on a catafalque. On both sides of her, apostles, clerical dignitaries, and seers of oracles stand. One of the apostles holds a censer in his hand, whereas the other people are portrayed leaning towards the bed in deep sorrow. Behind the bed, Jesus in an oval halo joins the gathering. Here, Christ holds a baby in his arms. This baby symbolically represents the soul of his mother. Around Jesus, in the upper zone of the big oval halo, we see angels singing. Above this, Ashrael, the angel of death, is flying, and on the right, two sky torches are climbing up with a great speed. From of the way people stand, from of the twist and folds of their garments, and finally, from their facial expressions, it is deduced that the scene is depicted with elaborate fineness and reality.

In this nave of the church, on the frontal surface of the rank of the apse, and on the right, we see the Virgin with the child Jesus in her arms. This panel of mosaics, which is framed like an icon, is partly in a bad shape. On the north wall of the apse, we find the mosaics of Jesus. This panel has also reached our era with considerable damage. On this panel, Jesus holds an open book in his hand. In this book, there is an inscription meaning "All those with great fatigue and under great burdens, come up to me; I shall give you peace".

The death scene of the Virgin in the main section (nave) of the Chora.

The death of the Virgin.

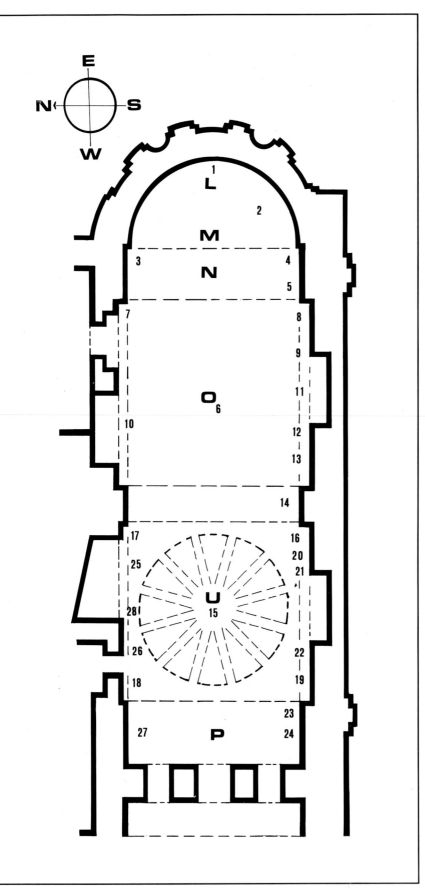

Plan of the Parecclesion

1- The Anastasis.

2- The church fathers.

3- The raising (resurrection) of the widow's son.

4- The healing of the daughter of Jairus.

5- The Virgin Elousa.

6- The Last Judgment.

7- Abraham and the beggar Lazarus on his lap

8- St. George

9- Rich man burning in Hell's fire.

10- Those entering Heaven and the Angel Seraphim with the semi-nude good thief.

11- Depiction of Andronikus II and his family, and the inscription and depiction above of Makarios Tornikes and his wife Eugenia.

12- The Bearing of the Ark of the Covenant.

13- St. Demetrius.

14- St. Theodore Tiro.

15- Mary and child Jesus with the twelve attending angels.

16- Four Gospel Writers (Hymnographers) : St. Cosmos.

17- Four Gospel Writers (Hymnographers) : St. John of Damascene.

18- Four Gospel Writers (Hymnographers) : St. Theophanes.

19- Four Gospel Writers (Hymnographers) : St. Joseph.

20- St. Theodore Stratelates.

21- King Solomon and the Israelites.

22- Placement into the temple of The Ark of the Covenant

23- The combat of an angel with the Asurians in the outskirts of Jerusalem.

24- St. Procopios, St. Sabas Stratelates.

25- Moses in the bushes.

26- Jacob's ladder and the angels.

27- Aaron and his sons carrying votive offerings, in front of the altar.

28- St. Samonas and Guiras.

Jesus Christ from the frescoes of the Anastasis.

The frescoes of the parecclesion

The annexed grave chapel, the Parecclesion, built by Metochites, lies alongside the church and ends with a wide arched apse. We reach here by passing through two narrow columns. The columns further ahead have more slender bodies, and carry elegant capitals. Light pours in from the windows of the dome at the middle of the nave. In the side chapel called the Parecclesion, on the marble slab placed on the arch at the right of the middle of the chapel, an inscription is found.

In the Parecclesion, there are four grave niches counter each other and two passages. The first two niches in the south and the north are embellished with pieces of marble ornaments belonging to earlier periods, and used again later on. At the first niche on the front, we find mosaics and frescoes of Mikhail Tornikes and his wife, who are buried here. The annexed chapel is divided into two parts by a marble freeze. At the bottom, the soldier saints are depicted. Important members of the church are portrayed in the apse.

Frescoes were most likely made by the masters who did the mosaics. At the first section of the chapel, when standing against the apse, one can see that many important scenes from the Old Testament are dealt with.

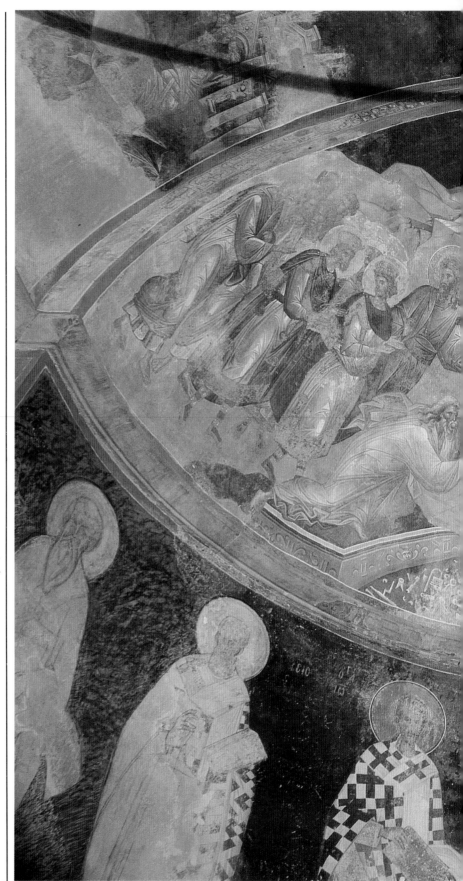

The magnificent Anastasis frescoes of the Parecclesion.

The Virgin Elousa.

Fresco of the Anastasis (1)

On the semi-dome of the apse, a symbolic subject such as Jesus being capable of saving his predecessors is dealt with. In the Anastasis fresco of unbelievable beauty Jesus, who has descended the after-life, and clad in a pure white robe, is seen pulling Adam and Eve out of their sarcophagi. Jesus is portrayed in a strong manner, within a frame ornamented with stars, around which light blue shades are dominant. Here, behind Adam, who is extracted from the sarcophagus by Jesus, stands John the Baptist. The panel, which continues towards the left contains the portraits of king-apostles. On the right side of the panel, we see Cain attired in a slightly greenish robe and holding his sceptre with a twisted end. He stands in front of the people seen behind Eve. Under the feet of Jesus stand the gates of hell, torn into pieces, and we see the black guard of Hades, his hands hand-cuffed and taken prisoner. The descending of Jesus to Hades, after his crucification and prior to his ascending into Heaven, is in existence in Byzantine art. This subject has been dealt with frequently in Western art. We see on top of the arch of the apse, an angel in medallion and six saints of the church, below the anastasis fresco. In the bema of the side walls of the apse, two miracles of Jesus are dealt with, facing each other. In the two frescoes which are similar, we see two miracles being performed, namely the raising (resurrection) of the daughter of Jairus on the right; and the raising of the son of a widow from Nain, on the left. Jesus goes to a town called Nain.

69 *The frescoes of the Anastasis and the saints.*

The frescoes of the Anastasis and the saints.

With him, there are his disciples and a crowd of people. When Christ reaches the gates of the town, he sees that the townspeople are in the process of the burial of the only son of a widow. Jesus feels pity for the woman and after saying to her, "Cry no more,", he walkes up and approaches the casket and touches it, saying "Rise young man." The youngster rises and sits. Then, he starts talking. (Luke 7: 11-15) Near the apse, on the southern wall, we see a fresco showing the Virgin holding tenderly and in affection the child Jesus in her arms (Virgin Elousa). Behind this, we see Saint George.

70

A detail from the Anastasis frescoes.
St. George.
A general view of the Parecclesion.

The last judgement scene (6)

After the magnificent Anastasias frescoes in the apse, the last judgement scene makes up one of the most crowded scenes of Byzantine art. Just at the middle of the panel, the figure of Jesus is found, sitting on a throne, and separated from the other figures by a halo surrounding him. Mary, on the left, and John the Baptist on the right are seen in a pause of asking Christ for intercession for humanity. On both sides, we see the twelve apostles seated on benches, and arch angels and group of angels in the background. Above these, just in the middle of the vault (flying buttress) a snail carried by an angel is seen, the snail representing the Paradise. This is the first time in Byzantine art that a snail representing the Paradise is being depicted. This figure is made up of a scroll of rolls carried by the flying angel, the rolls opening up, being tossed about, twisted and folded. Underneath the halo surrounding Jesus, stands an unoccupied throne and Adam and Eve kneeling down in reverence. Just below this, the scene depicting the discussion by the angels the sins of the souls. On the right side of the vault, we see figures of the sinners tied up to each other and being led to Hell's fire, escorted by Satan, as well as figures of sinners burned in Hell's fire. They are surrounded by souls represented as children. In the other sections of the vault, "Chrosus of the Chosen" surrounded by clouds, are making headway towards the middle, to the Last Judgement. Underneath the pendant, in which we see the rich man burning in the flames of Hell's fire, we see four panels in which nude figures are depicted as groups of big

St. Cosmos of the Four Hymnographers.

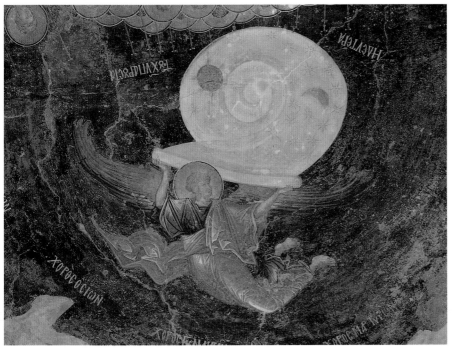

The Last Judgement scene.

The symbolical Heaven carried by an angel.

crowds. At the left, the semi-nude figure of the "good thief" is supervising the entrace into Heaven (paradise) of the chosen. In paradise, we see the partly damaged figure of the Virgin among the trees and angels. Here, opposite the pendant the fresco depicting Abraham and Lazarus the begger on his lap comes into view. The two west pendants of the vault are very much damaged. The one on the left depicts the rendering of the dead by the sea and the earth, while two angels blow their horns; and the one on the right shows an angel beside a soul in the form of a child.

The Virgin and the attendant twelve angels in the dome

The dome of the Parecclesion is ornamented by the figures of the Virgin and the attendant twelve angels. With the light pouring from the twelve windows, the figures of the Virgin and the surrounding twelve angels are seen very clearly and gracefully.

The ornamented grooves coming out of the medallion in the middle, divide the dome into twelve sections, and an angel holding a spear is depicted in each section. Under these, the holy legend is depicted.

In the pendentives of the dome, we see the four gospel writers or four hymnographers, namely Saint Joseph the poet, Saint Cosmos, Saint Theophares and Saint John of Damascene. Below the dome, subjects from the Old Testament are depicted on the walls and arches.

Here at the left, on the northern wall we see Jacob's ladder on the two sides of a window, and below this, Jacob dreaming and the angels ascending and descending the ladder; and above the Virgin and the Child Jesus are presented in a medallion.

On the right, we see Moses among the burning bushes. In the bushes, we see the Virgin and Jesus in a medallion. An angel in the bushes addresses Moses, holding a veil in his hand.

Mary and the Child Jesus in the dome.

One of the angels surrounding the Virgin and the child Jesus in the medallion.

77   *Another angel surrounding the Virgin and the child Jesus.*

A little further ahead, the depiction of the Bearing of the Ark of the Covenant is seen, and its continuation is on the niche of the tomb on the southern wall under the dome. At the left of the window, we see King Solomon and the Israelites, and at the right, the placement at the temple of the Ark of the Covenant is depicted. Aside these, we see the combat of an angel with the Asurians near the outskirts of Jerusalem. This is within the arch and has survived until our age, only being partly damaged. On the left of the arch, above the column at the entrance to the Parecclesion, we see Aaron and his sons in front of an altar,

A general view of the Kariye Museum.

St. Procopius - St. Stratelates.

presenting the votive offerings that they were carrying in their hands. The frescoes in the other half of the column have deteriorated. The blank spaces are filled with the frescoes of warriors holding spears and shields. There are some more frescoes here in the passage leading to the nave, in the side niches of the apse and in the annex with the northern galleries, but most of them are badly deteriorated. These parts are closed to visitors.

The Anastasis and the scenes of the Last Judgement.

PUBLICATIONS LIST

- **TURKEY (LITTLE FORMAT)**
  (In English, German, French)

- **TOURISTIC GUIDE OF TURKEY**
  (In English, French, German, Japanese, Turkish)

- **TREASURES OF TRUKEY (LARGE FORMAT)**
  (In English, French, German, Italian, Spanish)

- **THE CITY OF TWO CONTINENTS, ISTANBUL**
  (In English, French, German, Italian, Spanish)

- **TREASURES OF ISTANBUL (LARGE FORMAT)**
  (In English, French, German)

- **THE TOPKAPI PALACE (LITTLE FORMAT)**
  (In English, French, German, Italian, Spanish, Japanese)

- **THE TOPKAPI PALACE (LARGE FORMAT)**
  (In English, French, German)

- **PAMUKKALE - HIERAPOLIS**
  (In English, French, German, Italian, Spanish, Swedish, Dutch)

- **CAPPADOCIA**
  (In English, French, German, Italian, Spanish)

- **EPHESUS, KUŞADASI, PRIENE, MILET, DIDYMA**
  (In English, French, German)

- **MARMARIS - BODRUM**
  (In English, French, German)

- **GUIDE TO EASTERN TURKEY**
  (In English, French, German)

- **THE CRYSTAL - CLEAR WATERS OF THE TURQUOISE COAST - THE BLUE VOYAGE**
  (In English)

- **ANTALYA**
  (In English, French, German, Italian)

- **MEVLANA AND THE MEVLANA MUSEUM**
  (In English, French, German)

- **THE EVOLUTION OF TURKISH ART AND ARCHITECTURE** (In English)

- **CHORA**
  (In English, French, German)

- **TURKISH CARPET ART**
  (In English, French, German)

- **THE BLUE SAILING (LARGE FORMAT)**
  (In English)

- **ISTANBUL (LITTLE FORMAT)**
  (In English, French, German)

İLHAN AKŞİT

İlhan Akşit was born in Denizli in 1940. He graduated as an archaeologist in 1965. When he was assigned to a post related to the excavation of Aphrodisias.

He was director of the Çanakkale - Troy Museum between 1968-1976, during which time the replica of the Trojan horse we now see on the site was constructed. He directed the excavation of the Chryse Apollo temple over a period of five years. From 1976-1978, the author acted as director of the Underwater Archaeology Museum, Bodrum and was appointed Director of National Palaces in 1978.

During his directorship, the author was responsible for the restoration and reopeninig of these palaces to the public after an extended period of closure. In 1982 the retired from his post to take up a career as an author of popular books on Turkish archaeology and tourism.

He has nearly 3 titles to his credit to date, including 'The Story of Troy', 'The Civilizatons of Anatolia', 'The Blue Journey', 'Istanbul', and The Hititites'.